Badger Publishing Limited
Oldmedow Road,
Hardwick Industrial Estate,
King's Lynn PE30 4JJ
Telephone: 01553 816083

www.badgerlearning.co.uk

4 6 8 10 9 7 5 3

Chocolate Unwrapped ISBN 978-1-78837-568-9

Text © Tim Collins 2021
Complete work © Badger Publishing Limited 2021

KU-101-970

Publishing Developer: Sarah Capon
Editor: Claire Morgan
Copyeditor: Cheryl Lanyon
Designer: Adam Wilmott
Cover design: Shaun Page

Photos: Cover Image: Shulevskyy Volodymyr/Shutterstock.com
Page 4: Valentyn Volkov/Shutterstock.com
Page 5: Bridgeman Images
Page 6: FLHC51/Alamy Stock Photo
Page 7: guentermanaus/Shutterstock.com, benjawan asawalapsakul/Shutterstock.com,
        Picture Partners/Shutterstock.com
Page 8: Olinchuk/Shutterstock.com, dowraik/Shutterstock.com
Page 9: Kingfajr/Shutterstock.com
Page 10: Sea Wave/ Shutterstock.com
Page 11: Elzbieta Sekowska/ Shutterstock.com
Page 12: Shaun Page, Africa Studio/Shutterstock.com
Page 13: Yogi Black/Alamy Stock Photo
Page 14: Amoret Tanner /Alamy Stock Photo, © Look and Learn / Bridgeman Images
Page 15: robtek/Shutterstock.com
Page 16: PA Images / Alamy Stock Photo
Page 17: Pras Nazri/Shutterstock.com
Page 18: Shaun Page
Page 19: Pierre-Yves Babelon/Shutterstock.com
Page 20: REUTERS / Alamy Stock Photo
Page 21: Darios/Shutterstock.com
Page 22: chrisdorney/Shutterstock.com
Page 23: chrisdorney/Shutterstock.com
Page 24: Abramova Elena/Shutterstock.com
Page 25: Billion Photos/Shutterstock.com, SAPhotog/Shutterstock.com
Page 27: irin-k/Shutterstock.com
Page 28: Ermolaev Alexander/Shutterstock.com
Page 29: Andrew Makedonski/Shutterstock.com

Attempts to contact all copyright holders have been made.
If any omitted would care to contact Badger Learning, we will be happy to make appropriate arrangements.

CHOCOLATE UNWRAPPED

TIM COLLINS

CHOCOLATE UNWRAPPED

Contents

Badger

1. THE ORIGINS OF CHOCOLATE

We might think of chocolate as a modern snack, but it has actually been around for thousands of years. It was enjoyed in the Americas long before it reached Europe and the rest of the world.

Words highlighted in this colour are in the glossary on page 30

People who lived in Mexico and Central America hundreds of years ago, such as the Maya and the Aztecs, made a cold, frothy drink by crushing the beans of the cacao (ka-kay-oh) tree and mixing them with water. They sometimes added chilli or vanilla for flavour.

They called it 'xocolatl' (choc-o-la-tull) which is probably where the word 'chocolate' comes from. But this drink had a bitter taste and was very different from the sweet chocolate we know today.

Cacao pod with beans inside

Chocolate was very important to both the Maya and the Aztecs. They drank it for energy but also used it as medicine for lots of different illnesses.

The Maya used it in religious ceremonies. Many carvings, drinking cups and **manuscripts** have been found that show their gods next to cacao trees. One vase even shows the head of a god growing out of a cacao tree.

The Aztecs believed chocolate was only meant for the gods. One of their gods, Quetzalcoatl (ket-zal-ko-a-tull), made the other gods angry by stealing the cacao tree and showing humans how to make the special drink.

Quetzalcoatl,
the 'chocolate god'

Cacao beans were so **valuable** to the Aztecs that they used them as money. They could trade beans for food or clothing. We have all heard the saying, 'money doesn't grow on trees', but in this case it was true!

Maya chocolate recipe

1. Remove the pods from a cacao tree and take out the cacao beans.

2. Keep the cacao beans in their white pulp and leave them for a few days. They will ferment (start to break down), turning brown.

3. Dry the beans in the sun for a week. They will turn a darker brown.

4. Roast the beans in a clay pot, then peel away their shells.

5. Grind what is left into a paste.

6. Mix the paste with water.

7. Add a crushed chilli pepper.

8. Pour the mixture back and forth between two cups to make it frothy. Then it's ready!

2. CHOCOLATE GETS SWEET

European explorers first began to visit South America and set up **colonies** in the late 1400s. The Italian explorer Christopher Columbus reached the Caribbean in 1492.

Columbus was one of the first Europeans to see cacao beans when he and his crew stole a canoe of goods from some Mayan traders. They noticed that the traders were careful to pick up any dropped cacao beans, which showed they were valuable.

In 1519, Spanish explorer Hernán Cortés and his crew arrived on the coast of Mexico. They had found the home of the Aztecs, and made their way to a city ruled by Montezuma II.

Montezuma was friendly to Cortés and his crew, and gave them many valuable gifts, including their special chocolate drink. However, things did not stay friendly for long, and the Spanish soon took over the city, killing many Aztecs and making others their slaves. They forced the Aztecs to hand over their valuable cacao beans so that they could make their own chocolate drink.

The drink was taken to Spain, where it was changed forever. No one knows exactly where it happened or who did it, but someone added sugar to the mix and it became much more like the drink we know today.

Prince Philip of Spain liked the drink and it became
very fashionable with rich people. **Settlers** in the
Spanish colonies set
up cacao farms, or
plantations, so the
beans could be
harvested and sent
back to Spain.
Local people were
forced to work on
these farms, but
they soon became
tired and sick, and
many died.

The Spanish managed to keep chocolate to themselves
for nearly 100 years. It wasn't until the 1700s that
chocolate became popular in places like England and
France too.

For a while, chocolate remained a drink for the rich.
It had to be made by hand and it was very expensive.
This changed in the early 1800s.

In 1828, a Dutch chemist called Casparus van Houten and his son, Conrad, invented the cocoa press. It was a powerful machine that separated the fat from cacao beans, leaving behind a fine powder. The name was then changed from **cacao** to **cocoa** (co-co). No one knows why!

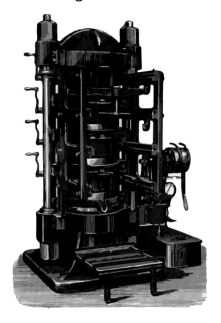

The fat was called **cocoa butter**.

The powder was called **cocoa powder**.

It was easy and cheap to make chocolate with cocoa powder, and it became a drink for everyone, not just those with lots of money.

Some people added dried milk to the powder, creating the first milk chocolate. The sweet, milky drink we enjoy today had arrived.

3. THE CHOCOLATE BAR

The Bristol Post

September 4th 1847

New Chocolate Sensation!

Mr Joseph Storrs Fry from Bristol has revealed his exciting new invention — chocolate that you can eat! There's no need for a cup with Mr Fry's 'chocolate bar'. You simply unwrap it and tuck in. Which unlikely drink will these inventors turn into food next? Milk? Lemonade? Tea?

Fry's chocolate factory in Bristol

Fry's mixed together sugar, cocoa powder and melted cocoa butter to form long, thin bars. They were very popular, and Fry's became the biggest chocolate-makers in the world.

Other companies such as Cadbury's, Terry's and Rowntree's brought out their own bars and soon everyone was eating chocolate.

In the 1870s, the Cadbury brothers bought some farmland near Birmingham to create a factory and a special village for their workers. It had lots of green spaces and nice, **affordable** housing. It was made so the workers could lead happier, healthier lives. They named it Bournville.

Bournville Works

THE FACTORY IN A GARDEN
BOURNVILLE

It is important that Food Products should be manufactured under clean and healthy conditions.
This essential has been fully observed at Bournville where every detail to promote cleanliness and the good health of the workers has been considered. Such ideal conditions ensure ideal productions.

CADBURY'S
COCOA & CHOCOLATES
are
"The very finest products." *Med Mag.*
MADE AT BOURNVILLE

At first, chocolate bars were made of dark chocolate. In the 1870s, Swiss chocolatiers (the French word for 'chocolate-makers') added powdered milk to create milk chocolate bars. In 1905, Cadbury's introduced the 'Dairy Milk' bar. It is still a bestseller to this day.

The 'combination bar' also took off in the late 1800s. Fry's introduced the 'Chocolate Cream' in 1866, which had a sweet, creamy filling instead of being solid chocolate. Soon all the chocolate companies were adding things such as nuts, raisins and wafers to their bars.

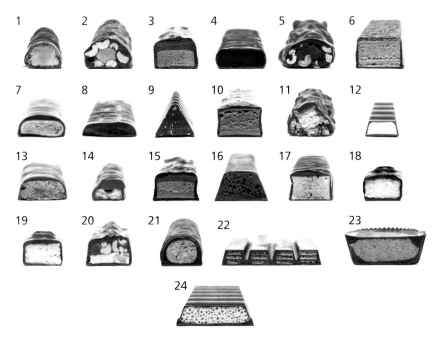

Can you work out which is which? Answers on page 31. Don't cheat!

WOW! facts

The world's heaviest chocolate bar was created by Thorntons in Alfreton, Derbyshire in 2011. It weighed 5792.50 kilograms, which is about the same as a large African elephant!

4. THE CHOCOLATE INDUSTRY

Chocolate is one of the best-loved foods in the world today. As well as being popular as a drink and in bars, it's used as flavouring in everything from cakes to pasta and even cheese! Over four million tonnes of cacao beans are produced every year to keep up with the demand.

Would you try chocolate and cheese on toast?

But growing cacao trees is not easy. They need protection from weather, diseases and pests.

They need hot weather, lots of rain and to be planted under tall trees. There are only a few places close to the equator, where it's hottest, where they can be grown. They are shown in different colours on this map:

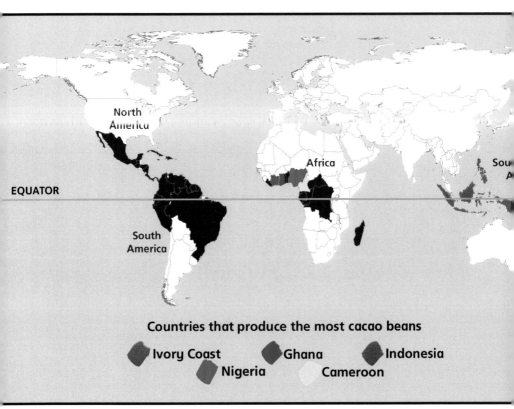

North America

Africa

Sou A

EQUATOR

South America

Countries that produce the most cacao beans

Ivory Coast　　Ghana　　Indonesia

Nigeria　　Cameroon

A man prepares cacao beans for fermenting

Since chocolate first came to Europe it has been easy for chocolate lovers not to know or think about the terrible price paid by people forced to work as slaves on cacao plantations.

Today, there is still a dark side to this work.

Many cacao farms still use child labour. Although it is against the law for children to work on the plantations, some estimates suggest that over two million of them still do. They are often made to use dangerous **machetes** and carry heavy sacks of cacao pods.

The world's biggest chocolate companies have promised not to use any cacao farmed by children, but they do not always know where their supplies come from. Stopping child labour is the biggest challenge facing the chocolate industry today.

Another challenge is making sure that chocolate is Fair Trade. If you want to help the people on cacao farms, you could choose to buy Fair Trade chocolate. This means the farmers get a higher price for their chocolate, and the workers have better conditions.

3D printers now make it easy to form chocolate into unusual or tricky shapes. They could even make a **mould** of your face!

5. THE CHOCOLATE TOP FIVE

A survey done by the British Heart Foundation in 2020 found that these five chocolate bars are the best-loved in the UK. Which is your favourite?

Number one: Snickers

Snickers was voted the most popular bar. This is no surprise, as it's the bestselling bar in the world. It was first sold in 1930 by the Mars Company, and was named after the Mars family's favourite horse.

The bar used to be called 'Marathon' in the UK, but it was changed to Snickers in 1990 so it had the same name all over the world.

Number two: Dairy Milk

Cadbury's sold their first milk chocolate bar in 1905, and it was a huge success.

They soon added their famous purple packaging and the promise that each bar contained 'a glass and a half' of milk.

Can you spot the Fair Trade logo?
It means the cacao farmers got a fairer
deal for the beans that went into this chocolate.

The Cadbury's factory in Bourneville near Birmingham produces 234 million bars of Dairy Milk every year. Workers are allowed to eat as much as they want! See more on the Bournville factory on page 14.

Number three: Galaxy

Galaxy is a milk chocolate bar that was first made in 1960 by the Mars Company. It was so popular that they changed the names of two other Mars products, Minstrels and Ripple, to 'Galaxy Minstrels' and 'Galaxy Ripple'.

Galaxy aims its advertising at women, while Mars bars are aimed at men, based on what studies say they prefer. But of course we know everyone is different!

Three ways that the Galaxy bar is aimed at women:

- lighter colours
- less chunky-looking than a Mars bar
- words like 'smooth' make it seem like a special treat, rather than something to fill you up.

Number four: Bounty

Bounty is a chocolate bar with a coconut filling that was first sold by the Mars Company in 1951. You can choose between a milk chocolate bar in a blue wrapper or a dark chocolate bar in a red wrapper.

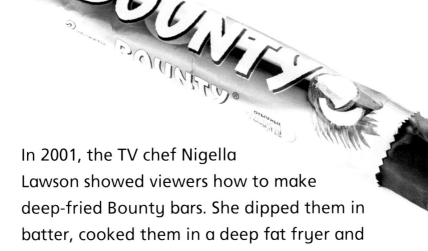

In 2001, the TV chef Nigella Lawson showed viewers how to make deep-fried Bounty bars. She dipped them in batter, cooked them in a deep fat fryer and served them with pineapple. Definitely not a healthy snack!

WOW! facts

There have been a few different flavours of Bounty in the past. A mango flavour was sold in Europe, a pineapple flavour was sold in Russia and a cherry flavour was sold in Australia.

Number five: Kit Kat

Kit Kats were launched in 1935, though they were called 'Rowntree's Chocolate Crisp' for the first two years.

Strange flavours of Kit Kat are popular in Japan. Over 300 different ones have been sold, including green tea, wasabi and melon. Would you eat a melon Kit Kat?

The fastest time to eat a Kit Kat with no hands is 22.52 seconds. Do you think you could beat that?

6. IS CHOCOLATE GOOD FOR YOU?

People often say that chocolate is bad for your health. But is this true?

Chocolate contains fat and sugar, and is high in calories. It can cause tooth decay and make you gain weight.

But that doesn't mean you should never eat it. As long as you eat plenty of fruit, vegetables and high-fibre foods as well, it's fine to enjoy chocolate now and again. Brushing your teeth will fight tooth decay and regular exercise will help you stay fit

A British Heart Foundation survey found that the average British person eats 7560 chocolate bars in their lifetime. Just don't try to eat them all at once!

The good news is that some scientists believe chocolate could actually be good for you.

Scientists think that dark chocolate might lower your **blood pressure**, protect your heart or even improve your memory.

But a lot more research is needed before we can be sure how much chocolate is actually good for you. Dreams of eating just chocolate all day are sadly never going to come true!

Warning — chocolate can poison you! That's because of one of the chemicals in it. But you would have to eat a huge amount to get a deadly dose. In fact, you'd have to eat around 40 kilograms of milk chocolate in one go. That's about 1333 Dairy Milk bars!

But take care. Animals can be poisoned by much smaller amounts of chocolate, which is why you should never let your dog eat it.

Some people get to eat chocolate as their job! Chocolate tasters are paid to try out new products before they reach the shops.

The author Roald Dahl was a chocolate taster for Cadbury's, which is how he got the idea for his book *Charlie and the Chocolate Factory*.

GLOSSARY

affordable — if something is affordable, most people have enough money to buy it. Affordable housing is homes that people who don't have much money are able to buy.

blood pressure — a measure of how much force your heart uses to pump blood around your body. If your blood pressure is higher or lower than normal it can make you ill. Your diet can affect your blood pressure.

colonies — a colony is a country or area that is ruled by another country; many people from the ruling country may settle there (see **settlers** below).

machetes — a machete is a wide, heavy knife that can be used as a tool or a weapon.

manuscripts — very old books or documents written by hand.

mould — a hollow shape you can pour a liquid into. When the liquid cools and goes solid you can take it out and it keeps the shape of the mould.

settlers — people who move to live in a new country, often a colony (see **colonies** above).

valuable — worth a lot of money; or very important to someone for another reason.

Questions

What did the Maya and Aztecs add to chocolate for flavour? (*page 4*)

Which Italian explorer arrived in the Caribbean in 1492? (*page 9*)

In which year was Fry's Chocolate Cream first sold? (*page 15*)

What is the biggest challenge facing the chocolate industry today? (*page 20*)

What is the bestselling chocolate bar in the world? (*page 21*)

In which country are melon Kit Kats sold? (*page 25*)

Answers for page 15:

1. Kinder Bueno	9. Toblerone	18. Dark Bounty
2. Reese's Nutrageous	10. Milky Way	19. Bounty
3. Mars Bar	11. Lion Bar	20. Snickers
4. Turkish Delight	12. Kinder Chocolate	21. Star Bar
5. Picnic	13. Fudge	22. Kit Kat
6. Tunnock's Chocolate Caramel Wafer	14. Twix	23. Reese's Peanut Butter Cup
7. Chomp	15. Mars Dark	24. Mint Aero
8. Daim	16. Wispa	
	17. Crunchie	

INDEX